M000247460

Ouch!
What Happens When a Bone Breaks or a Muscle Tears

John Manos

Contents

Rigby
A Harcourt Achieve Imprint

www.Rigby.com
1-800-531-5015

Chapter 1: How We Move

Do you know what happens when you run, jump, or throw a ball? Every time you move, two of your body's systems are working together. These systems are your skeletal system—your bones—and your muscular system—your muscles.

Because your bones cannot move on their own, your muscles pull on them to make you move. And because your muscles need to pull on something to be able to make you move, your muscles are attached to your bones. If these two body systems aren't working together, you can't sit in a chair or hold a pencil between your fingers!

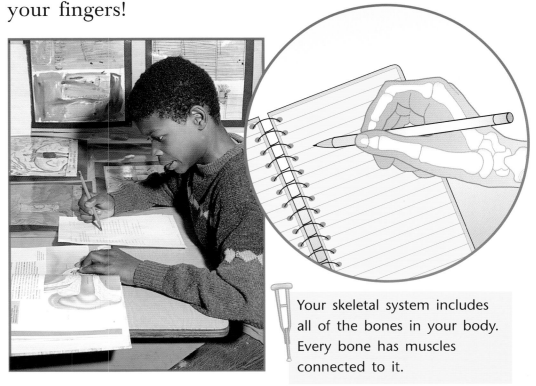

Your skeletal system includes all of the bones in your body. Every bone has muscles connected to it.

You can control the muscles in your muscular system. Try it yourself. Shrug your shoulders, like you don't know the answer to a question. Wave your hand as if you are saying good-bye to a friend. Your brain tells your muscular system how to work with your skeletal system, and that makes each of these movements possible. Thanks to these body systems, you can do things such as throw and catch a ball.

The muscles in your muscular system work with your bones to make you move. Most of your body's muscles are in the muscular system, but not all. You have muscles in your stomach, too!

4

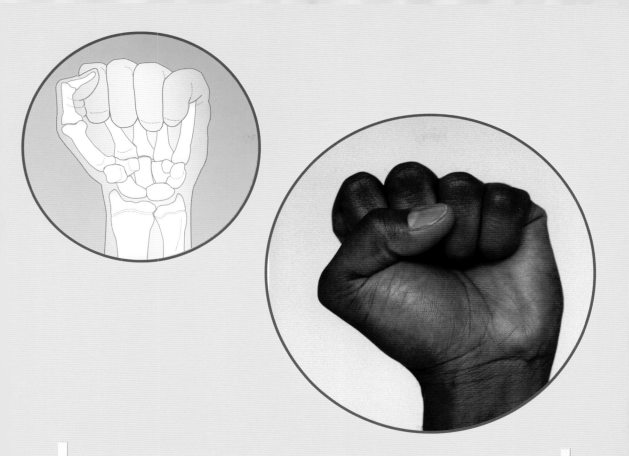

One good way to see how your muscular and skeletal systems work is this:

1. Make a fist with one hand.

2. Count from one to five, starting with your thumb and extending each finger in turn. See, you are telling your muscles to move your bones!

5

Chapter 2: All About Bones

If you tap your knee or press on the top of your head, the hard things you feel are bones! Your bones help you to stand up and to move around. Bones are the hard parts of your body that protect the inside of your body and support you. Without bones, you would have no shape!

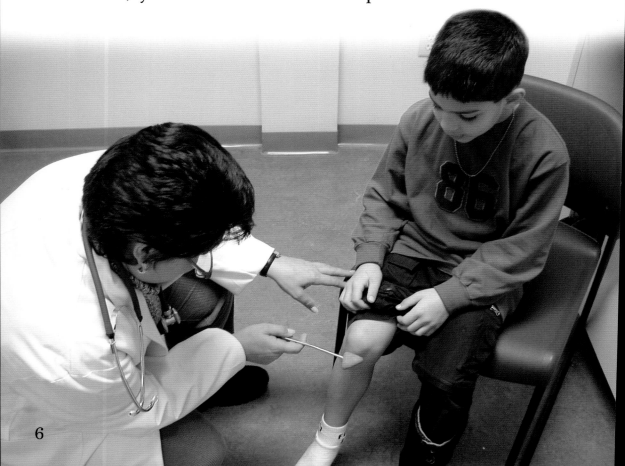

Even though your bones are hard, they are constantly changing. Your bones are a lot like your skin because they are breaking down and regrowing all the time. Like your skin, your bones are made of **cells** that are fed by your blood. Bones also are made of **minerals,** especially calcium.

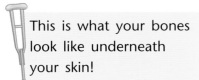
This is what your bones look like underneath your skin!

You have 206 bones in your body, including the tiny bones inside your ear and the long, thick bone in your thigh.

Your bones are strong, but they can break! Sometimes people break a bone when they fall down. For example, if people slip on an icy sidewalk or trip when they are running, they will probably hold their hands in front of them to keep their bodies from hitting the ground. However, if a person's hands hit the ground very hard, that person might break the thin bones in the lower part of his or her arm. Most people will break two bones during their lifetime.

Bones don't always break into two pieces like dry sticks would. Broken bones—also called **fractures**—break in many different ways. When some fractures happen, the bone cracks a little on one side, but it doesn't break all the way through. When other fractures happen, the bone is crushed into several pieces. Some types of fractures are more serious than others, but all of them will heal if properly treated by a doctor.

Which Bones Break the Most?

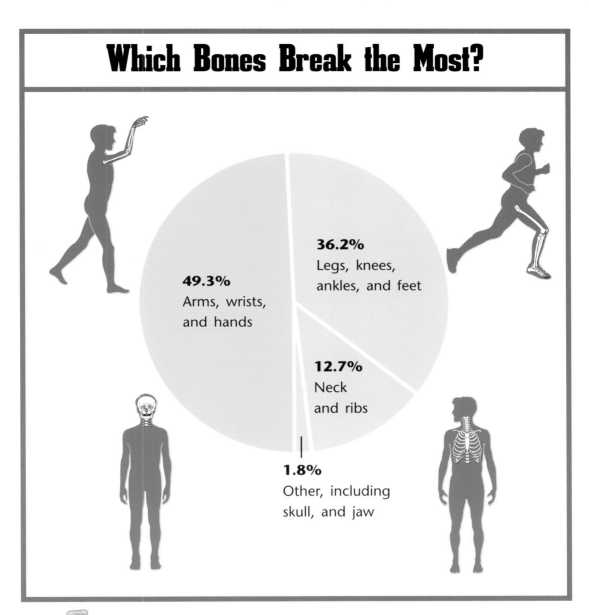

36.2%
Legs, knees,
ankles, and feet

49.3%
Arms, wrists,
and hands

12.7%
Neck
and ribs

1.8%
Other, including
skull, and jaw

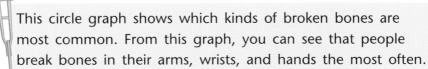

This circle graph shows which kinds of broken bones are most common. From this graph, you can see that people break bones in their arms, wrists, and hands the most often.

Chapter 3: How a Broken Bone Is Fixed

Imagine that you are riding bikes with your friend. Just as you are turning into your driveway, his tires begin to skid, and he falls off his bike and onto the sidewalk. You hear a loud snapping noise as his arm strikes the concrete, and he has tears in his eyes. He tells you that he feels dizzy and it's difficult for him to move his arm. It's already swollen as well as very sore.

When someone is hurt, get to a phone and dial 9-1-1!

Here are five things you should do if someone you know breaks a bone:

1. **1.** Stay calm. You don't want to scare your hurt friend.
2. **2.** Tell your friend not to move. Moving will hurt your friend more, and it might make the broken bone worse.
3. **3.** Make sure your friend is as comfortable as possible.
4. **4.** Find an adult to help your friend.
5. **5.** Call 9-1-1 for emergency help.

If you think your friend's bone is broken, the most important thing to do is to keep the bone still while you are waiting for the ambulance. The ambulance workers might put something around the broken bone to keep it from moving before taking your friend to the hospital.

The doctor in the emergency room will do several things to help your friend. First the doctor will ask your friend what he was doing when he hurt himself. This will help the doctor figure out what kind of fracture your friend may have.

Next the doctor will look at your friend's arm and touch it. The doctor might ask him to move his fingers or his hand. Usually an **X-ray** will then be taken of the arm. X-rays are photographs of bones inside the body. X-rays help a doctor find out where a bone is broken and how bad the fracture is.

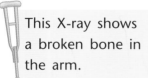

This X-ray shows a broken bone in the arm.

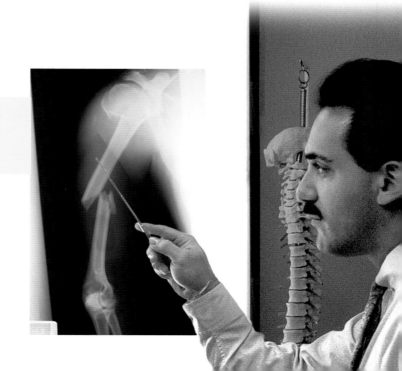

If your friend has a complete fracture, meaning the bone has broken into two pieces, the doctor will carefully move the arm so that the ends of the broken bone are in the right place again. Finally the doctor will put your friend's arm in a cast or a **splint** to keep the arm from moving.

A splint is a wrapping used to keep a broken bone from moving. Sometimes, when an arm is very swollen, a splint may be used at first. Once the arm isn't swollen anymore, a cast may replace the splint. A cast fits over a broken bone to help that bone heal.

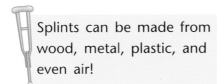
Splints can be made from wood, metal, plastic, and even air!

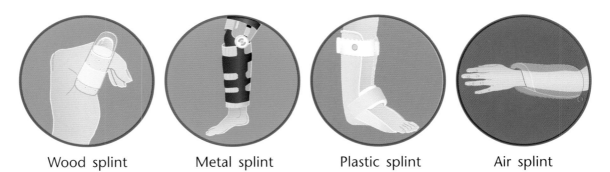

Wood splint   Metal splint   Plastic splint   Air splint

How Are Casts Made?

Casts can be made of either plaster or fiberglass. Both plaster and fiberglass casts are made in the same way.

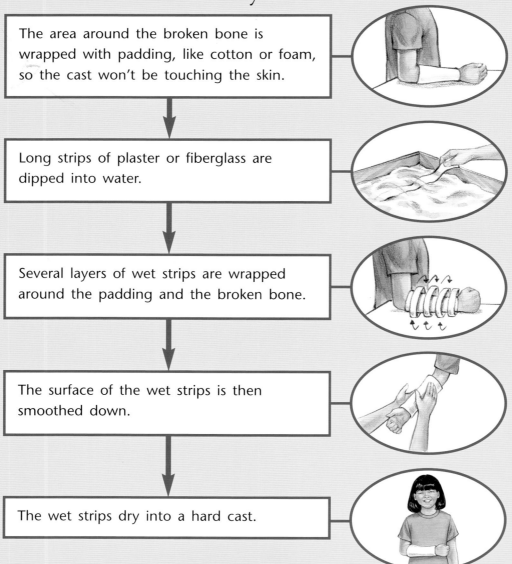

The area around the broken bone is wrapped with padding, like cotton or foam, so the cast won't be touching the skin.

Long strips of plaster or fiberglass are dipped into water.

Several layers of wet strips are wrapped around the padding and the broken bone.

The surface of the wet strips is then smoothed down.

The wet strips dry into a hard cast.

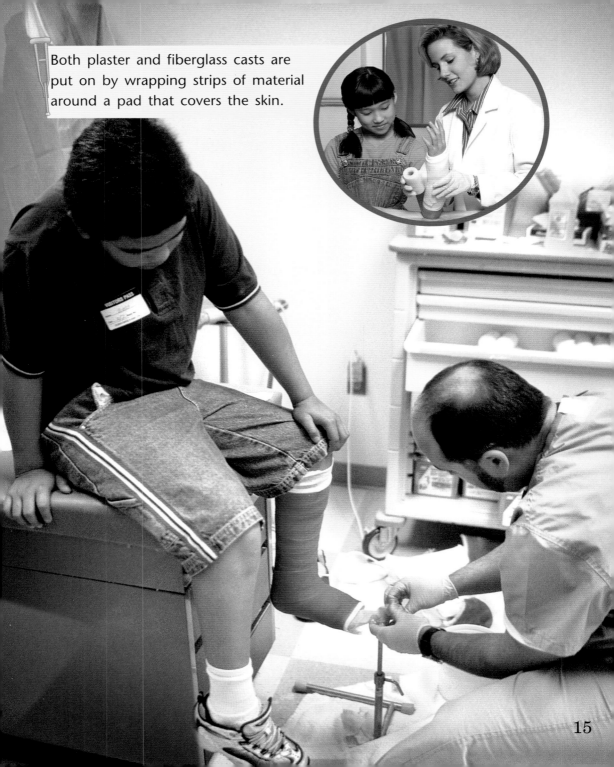

Both plaster and fiberglass casts are put on by wrapping strips of material around a pad that covers the skin.

15

Chapter 4: How Bones Heal

When your skin is cut, it can heal itself. Your bones can heal themselves, too. Here's how it happens:

1. Soon after a bone breaks, the bone starts to grow new cells.

2. Tiny blood vessels grow to rebuild the broken bone.

3. New cells grow into and over the fracture, forming a small lump.

4. After the bone is healed, the lump gets smaller and smaller.

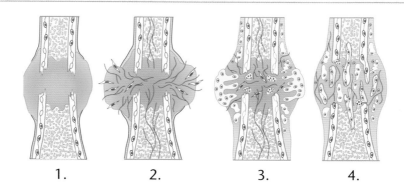

1.   2.   3.   4.

Broken bones in children, who are still growing, heal much more quickly than broken bones in adults. A fracture that might take six weeks to heal in an adult might heal in just three or four weeks in a child.

Bones can heal themselves just like a cut on your arm will heal itself. Once a bone is completely healed, a doctor will remove the cast.

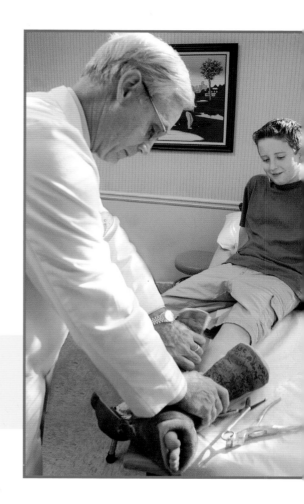

How long it takes for a fracture to heal—and how long a person will wear a cast or a splint—depends on which bone is broken and how bad the fracture is. For example, if a ball hits the end of your friend's finger and causes a small fracture, she will wear a splint for ten days to three weeks. If she has a fracture in her lower arm, she will probably wear a cast for four to six weeks. But if she breaks the long, thick bone in her thigh, she may be in a cast for three to six months!

Different types of casts and splints help many kinds of broken bones heal.

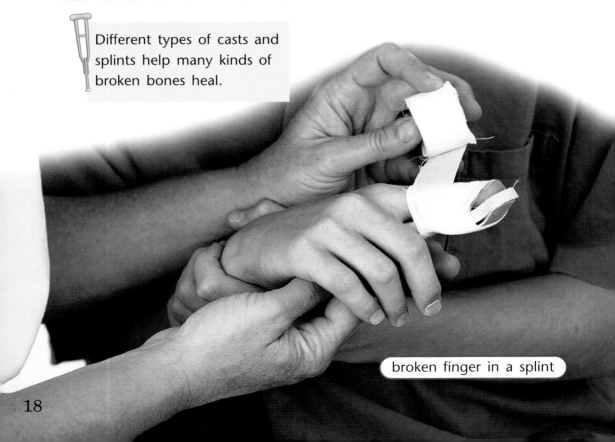

broken finger in a splint

18

How Long Will It Take a Broken Bone to Heal?

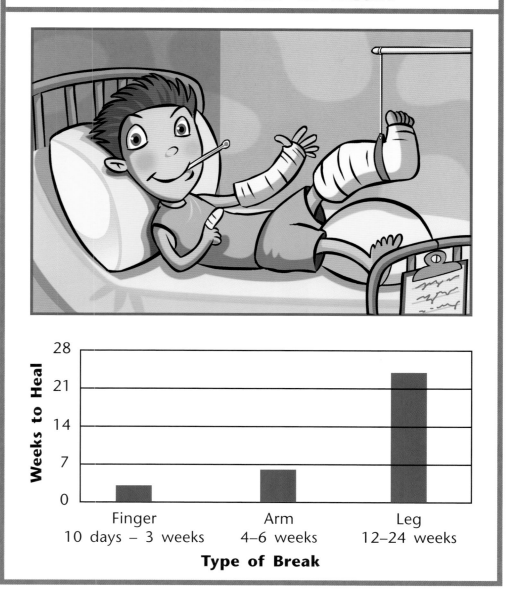

Weeks to Heal

28
21
14
7
0

Finger
10 days – 3 weeks

Arm
4–6 weeks

Leg
12–24 weeks

Type of Break

Chapter 5: All About Muscles

Feel the upper part of your arm. The thick part that you can squeeze beneath your skin is muscle. It isn't hard like your bones, is it? You can pinch your muscles, and you can move them around a little bit. But your muscles aren't completely soft, either.

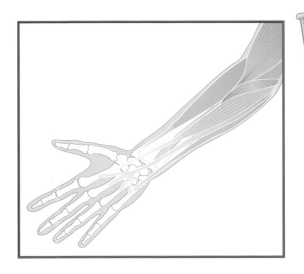

All of the muscles you can see and feel from the outside of your body are part of your muscular system. Even though your body has over 600 different muscles, doctors have particular names for only about 240 of them!

You have almost 700 different muscles in your body, from the small muscles that move your eyes to the heavy, strong muscles in your thighs. Like your bones, your muscles are made of cells, and these groups of cells, together, make up your muscle fibers. Each muscle in your body has between 10,000 and 500,000 fibers in it!

These muscle fibers are connected to your bones by tough, bendable tissues called tendons. Bend your arm about halfway up toward your shoulder, and touch the inside of your elbow. You can feel a rope-like tendon there. When you move, your muscle fibers pull on a tendon, which then pulls on a bone.

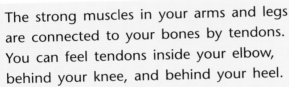

The strong muscles in your arms and legs are connected to your bones by tendons. You can feel tendons inside your elbow, behind your knee, and behind your heel.

Sometimes if a person twists or turns very fast or tries to lift a heavy weight, the muscle fibers can tear. Usually this isn't as bad as it sounds. If you fall down and scrape your knee, you have torn your skin. Most torn muscles are no worse than that. But like broken bones, some torn muscles are more serious than others.

 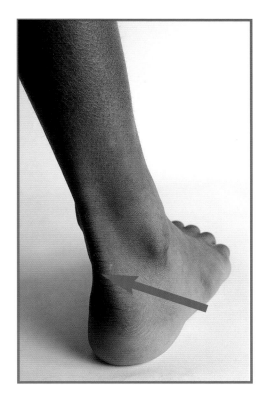

Chapter 6: How a Torn Muscle Is Fixed

Imagine that a baseball comes sailing over your friend's head. You don't think she can reach it, but she quickly throws her arm up into the air and makes an amazing catch! But what's wrong? Your friend is holding her arm to her side in pain.

She tells you that her arm feels like something stretched too far, and suddenly her muscle feels very weak. Perhaps the muscle can't move at all, and your friend may have heard a "pop," like when a bone breaks. There may even be a dent in the muscle that the doctor will be able to touch.

In the emergency room, the doctor will begin by examining your friend's torn muscle just as he or she would examine a broken bone—by asking your friend how the injury happened and by touching the injured muscle. X-rays are not usually needed. For most torn muscles, doctors tell people to just put ice on the injury so that it doesn't swell too much.

When a muscle tears, the muscle fibers actually pull apart and rip, sort of like when you get a cut in your skin.

If your friend has a minor muscle tear, all she needs to do is rest the muscle. If the tear is more serious, the doctor may put a bandage around the torn muscle so it cannot move. If the torn muscle is in your friend's arm or shoulder, the doctor may put her arm in a sling. But if it's a very serious injury, the doctor may put a cast on the muscle, just like with a broken bone. Sometimes the muscle needs to be reconnected to the tendon. When this is the case, a cast is always put on the injury.

For most torn muscles, all you need to do is rest the muscle, and it will heal itself. Sometimes doctors will use a brace or sling to be sure the muscle doesn't move while it heals.

Chapter 7: How Muscles Heal

Just like your skin and your bones, torn muscles heal themselves. If you slip and scrape your elbow, what happens? It may bleed, and then a scab forms on the scrape. Finally all that's left is a small scar.

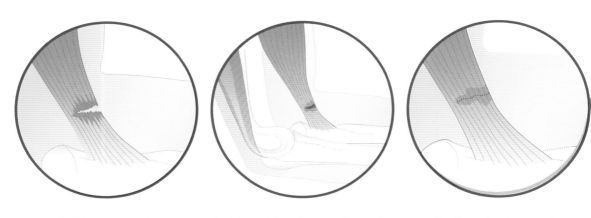

1. Torn muscle   **2.** New blood vessels and muscle fibers growing   **3.** Repaired muscle

Tears in your muscles heal themselves the same way that tears in your skin heal.

Sometimes when a muscle tears, the same thing happens. There may be some bleeding under the skin, a bruise may form, and the area may be tender when you touch it. Almost immediately new blood vessels and new muscle fibers begin to grow. Like when your skin heals from a cut, a torn muscle develops a small scar in the tissue. Therefore, doctors tell injured people to move a torn muscle again as soon as it doesn't hurt. This helps the muscle fibers grow, and it keeps a scar from blocking the movement of the new muscle fibers.

Usually a muscle tear heals in a few days, although you need to rest the muscle for at least a week or two.

For the worst muscle tears—and for badly broken bones—injured people often need to have **physical therapy** to get better after the cast is removed. During physical therapy, a trained person shows people who have been hurt how to do special exercises. These exercises help make the muscles strong again. There are even machines to move arms and legs to help make them easier to bend after they have been in casts.

Sometimes exercise is needed to help people get better after breaking a bone. People who have broken an arm bone may lift small weights. Other people might stretch their muscles to become strong again.

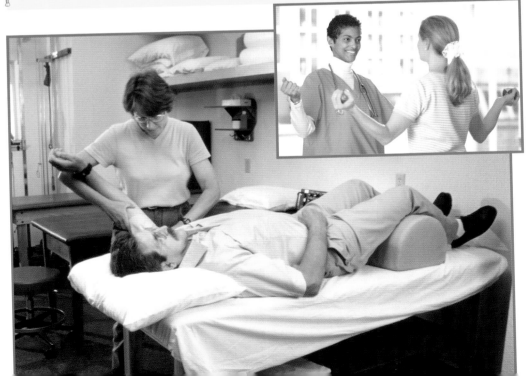

No matter what kind of muscle tear or broken bone a person has, it will heal itself if it's cared for and rested. The way our bodies heal is a wonderful thing!

Going to physical therapy can be just like exercising at a gym, but with special machines and trained people to help you get better after being hurt. Physical therapy can be a lot of fun!

Glossary

cell basic part of every living thing

fracture a broken bone

mineral a chemical found in the earth and in our foods that keeps our bodies healthy

physical therapy exercises to help an injured person get stronger

splint wrapping used to keep a broken bone from moving

X-ray a special ray that can make a photograph of bones and other things inside the body

Index